James Huniford
AT HOME

James Huniford
AT HOME

JAMES HUNIFORD
WITH STEPHEN TREFFINGER

Introduction by Pilar Viladas

THE MONACELLI PRESS

For Ava and Jack

Contents

Introduction

Pilar Viladas

JAMES HUNIFORD, known to all as Ford, creates rooms that are elegant, comfortable reflections of their owners' personalities and lifestyles, in a way that is both empathetic and intuitive. He blends old and new, high and low, formal and casual, with a skill that makes these contrasts look utterly effortless. Each of his projects is different, and each is an authentic response to its place and its occupants.

"I believe clients are drawn to my creative process, not a formula," he says. "I listen to them and create a home that corresponds to how they live. It's not about leaving my mark; it's about figuring out what needs to be done, taking chances, and creating something unique for them."

Summers on the St. Lawrence River and visits to historic houses on the Thousand Islands sparked Huniford's early interest in architecture. As a boy, he was "drawn to architecture and design by seeing things that were different from what I knew," and it was here that he first realized that things we often take for granted could be designed. They were, he recalls, "simple things, like a porch that was rounded, or cantilevered over the water," or "something beyond the simple purpose of a house," like the diamond-paned windows he saw in some of the buildings. Years later, Huniford added such a window to a bathroom in his own house in Bridgehampton on Long Island.

Never mind that it wasn't like the others in the house; for Huniford, the fact that it "changes the feeling of a room" was more important. "I'd much rather have pure and authentic," he says. "It doesn't have to match."

Huniford can pair an early twentieth-century chair by Josef Hoffmann with a modernist lamp by a 1940s ceramicist or works by A-list artists with found industrial objects that he treats as sculpture. While these "don't necessarily make sense on paper," he notes, "they have a thread, and when they're in the same environment, they work." In the same vein, Huniford doesn't always take a house's existing floor plan as gospel. In one case, he turned a dining room into a den, and placed a long trestle table at one end of the living room. "It's not the expected thing," he says. "I don't always play by the rules."

Nevertheless, Huniford's respect for context is a constant. A cozy, antiques-filled farmhouse in Connecticut; a sleek, modern Manhattan apartment; a Nashville house where traditional architecture contrasts with contemporary art; or a luxurious Park Avenue apartment—the spaces could not be more diverse. But Huniford's sensitivity to his surroundings—shaped by his travels as a young man to Europe, where he saw how architecture, art, and decorative arts "can co-exist across time periods, cultures, and styles"—results in an authenticity that runs through all his work. "My job is working with the context," he says. "I know that's what I really enjoy. I can't put into words how I achieve it, but it's something I conscientiously adhere to."

A hallmark of Huniford's approach is his collaborative relationship with his clients. He developed this skill as a founding partner of the firm Sills Huniford. But after going out on his own in 2008, he was able to give free rein to his intuitive, contextual approach. "I try to create the sensibility of the client, he says. "We talk about what home means to them and about creating a sense of calm and comfort. I talk about the opportunity that I see—which is often different from what might exist."

Many of Huniford's clients are art collectors, and he, too, is influenced by artists, as with Louise Nevelson's use of found objects in her wooden assemblages, the minimalist sculpture of Donald Judd, or Agnes Martin's rigorous paintings. Huniford might place a sculpture on a dining table rather than on a pedestal or put three pieces of art where there could be just one, so that no single piece is "that important." He mixes contemporary art with older works, and blue-chip pieces with humble ones.

"That's what makes a great space, that kind of freedom and flow," he says.

MAKING

"We chose Ford because he is approachable and came to the table with an open mind. We knew he could design a home that would reflect us, our family, and our needs. He loves a contemporary light fixture and a 1940s Italian sofa equally, the high mixed with the low. He has a point of view and an aesthetic, but not a cookie cutter formula. And everything isn't so precious. That speaks to our aesthetic. The architecture of our house is modern; Ford's aesthetic is warm and inviting. That's why it was a perfect match. We wanted to walk in and see color and light and texture. Ford guided us to exactly that."

—MELISSA SPOHLER

A

HOME

MOST WHO VISIT FORD HUNIFORD AT HIS WEEKEND HOME IN
Bridgehampton on Long Island don't ever cross the tiers of tall
sea grass that flank the stone path in the front yard. Nor do they
enter through the front door, where they would arrive into one of
the casual yet elegant sitting rooms, filled with sculptural furniture
covered in a variety of subtle textures and muted, neutral colors.
Rather, most guests pull into the gravel drive and arrive directly
into the kitchen, through a door near the garage.

Once inside, guests might be met, depending on the time
of day or the occasion, by their host and other guests arranging
flowers in tall, California art pottery vases or slicing vegetables for
the evening's dinner, or by his children eating lunch. A long trestle
table serves as part laboratory (buckets of unusual blooms and
greenery await), part worktable, and part informal dining area.

This is a perfect manifestation of Ford's personality: relaxed,
unpretentious, welcoming. It's not about hitting people over the head
with a grand entrance or catching their eye with sparkly finishes.
Design isn't about ego or ostentation. It's about creating a space in
which people can be who they are—albeit in an elevated way.

<< Tall French doors are so
dramatic they require bold
gestures to balance them.
A sculpture by Andrew Lord
in the garden and a French
campaign table from Villa
Fiorentina, a house designed
by Billy Baldwin, provide
interest inside and out.

> A vintage farm table that
can seat a large group is
at the heart of Huniford's
Bridgehampton house. From
here, food and flowers are
dispatched to the rooms
beyond. Found industrial
objects, such as the factory
molds on the wall, are
signature pieces, as are
large crocks of greenery.

On the Upper East Side, for instance, in the duplex of clients with whom he has worked for many years, Huniford created a design scheme that is grand—but not granny—to match their modern but uptown lifestyle. Arriving guests are able to peer into four rooms: an eccentric library with faux-bois walls, woodlands art, and a somewhat country vibe; a glamorous dining room with a hammered-brass-edged Louis XVI mahogany dining table, striped silk wallpaper, and embroidered linen curtains; a modern den in jewel tones; and an imperial (but not imperious) living room with gilding, marquetry, braiding, cording, brocades, and deeply tufted sofas. It feels like a collection of fine pieces assembled over time, stored in several attics for generations, and brought together at the perfect moment.

Effective design means eschewing a signature "look" that is easily recognizable. Instead it is more about representing the people who live there and creating a framework, one that can grow and adapt as the lives of the inhabitants change. A solid design shouldn't fall apart if the owner wants to change the fabric on an armchair five years on. As a result, Hunford is able to take on an impressive range of projects, from a rustic restored barn in upstate New York for an artist and her aging mother to a vast Manhattan loft for an agent.

Designing a home is a highly intimate process, based on a keen understanding of the those who will inhabit that house or apartment (and, in some cases, an office.) It's about translating the essence of a person, a couple, a family into furniture and lighting, yes, but also an overall sensibility.

In order to determine the perfect layout and decor, a few important questions must be answered. And sometimes challenged. Are they formal people who will benefit from a grand dining room? (Many believe they are, and then end up using it twice a year, spending the rest of their time in the kitchen.) Do they prefer open layouts with plenty of clear space, or intimate groupings that feel cocoon-like? Are they looking for more of a safe harbor or an entertainment hub. (The answer is, more often than not, a combination of both.) Ford's strength is in listening and intuiting, reading his clients, and combining various ingredients to provide a home that not only fulfills functional needs, but also one that provides comfort, refuge, utility—and certainly delight.

This Upper East Side dining room incorporates a complex interplay of bold modern art, regal elements such as striped silk wall covering, gilt chairs, and soft linen curtains. The landscape is by David Hockney.

> In this urban home on the Lower East Side of Manhattan, the clients, photographer Lonnie Duka and his wife, Melanie, wanted to stay away from bold colors and big design statements. A pale, neutral color scheme and rounded forms soften the industrial envelope. The photographs between the windows are by Duka. Furnishings include Barrow side chairs and Sinclair lamps from the Huniford Collection and a custom sofa.

>> Ariel Foxman and his husband, Brandon Cardet-Hernandez, were planning to have a child when Ford designed their apartment. The design has generous surfaces for Foxman's book and art collection—plus space to accommodate the "stuff" that comes with a newborn. Furniture in the dining area includes a Cortland table and benches from the Huniford Collection and a vintage sideboard.

>> Combinations of textures can create an unexpected rapport between furnishings. The sisal rug is nubby and casual, while the vintage armchairs upholstered in a botanical fabric are "old world" in the best possible way. Brass and wood shelves are refined and elegant. Lacquered coffee and side tables reflect the abundant light from the west-facing windows. The painting over the mantel is by Kathy Moss.

The artwork reads:

FOR
YOUR
IN
FOR
MATION WE
THE
PEOPLE
ARE
ALL
IMMIGRANTS

In the West Village home of Stephen Ferrara, the mood is elevated casual. The striped vintage kilims are Bohemian but tailored. The tiered raw-edge wood coffee table displays art books and pottery in front of a custom sofa. The painting is by Dan Miller.

> Huniford's Tribeca loft combines elements that are both rich and inviting. He is both a designer and a dad so although everything is impeccable, this is also a family room. An Italian wing-back chair covered in custom Chapas fabric faces a suite of nine drawings by Donald Judd from a series of sixteen. On the table beside the custom sofa is a bronze Giacometti lamp.

>> A portfolio manager wanted to minimize the environmental footprint in his Lower East Side apartment. This organic eden within the kinetic city uses milk-based paints and reclaimed barn wood—plus insulation that blocks electromagnetic frequencies—but does not hold back on sophistication. Above the raw-edge wood table, with built-in turntable from BDDW, is the Bond chandelier from the Huniford Collection.

∧ In a North Salem den, lively
patterns in brocade (sofa),
floral prints (armchair) and
stripes (Roman shades) maintain the eclectic Bloomsbury
vibe the owners wanted for
their weekend home. Ginger
jar lamps with Chinese
character stamp pattern and
contrasting shades add to the
spiritedness. The painting is
by Matvey Levenstein.

> A Damien Hirst Butterfly
print hangs above a custom
banquette in an Upper West
Side apartment.

< In the living room of a Nashville house, embossed faux eel-skin wallpaper and a carpet that evokes ancient Roman mosaic floors bring drama to the mix of furnishings, which includes custom armchairs and the Baxter sofa from the Huniford Collection. The table is lacquered goat-skin by Karl Springer and the scroll-back chair is by Jean-Michel Frank.

∧ In the Nashville master bedroom, a custom bed with headboard in Donghia velvet makes the high ceiling feel more intimate. Dusky white walls form a sensuous envelope that gives the room an opulent feeling. The lamp by Michael Taylor and a vintage rope-form settee from the 1930s covered in a navy glazed linen are glamorous and sculptural.

<< A bold wall sculpture by Claes Oldenburg lives peacefully among more traditional furnishings in this Katonah house. Rare cerused-oak Eyre de Lanux chairs upholstered in vanilla-colored horsehair anchor the seating area in front of a monumental desk and a Biedermeier cabinet.

> In a Connecticut guest bedroom, embroidery, prints, and stripes co-exist in harmony.

< Soho lofts of enormous size can be difficult to make feel intimate. Liberal use of reclaimed wood and a quartet of swiveling stools create a gathering place where groups can take part in the cooking or engage in close conversation.

∧ Kitchens do not have to be large hubs, especially in New York apartments, where space is at a premium. Here, a minimal marble island and a linear cooking and cabinetry area are efficient.

∧ In a West Village townhouse, there is an ingenious meeting of the contemporary, the classical, and the rustic in an elegantly shaped sofa covered in a custom Nantucket Looms fabric, a Giacometti plaster sculpture, and a nineteenth-century German architect's table.

> On the Upper West Side, bold prints in primary colors by Sol LeWitt are paired with a serene, traditional scheme of grays and beiges. A shagreen chest of drawers makes for unusual—and unusually useful—bedside table, while a custom bench at the foot of the bed is a perch for both books and people.

"The greatest feature in the apartment is the view of the Central Park reservoir. Ford made a beautiful window seat, and there's nothing better than sitting there with a cup of tea in the morning or a glass of wine at night and watching the sky change colors. He also maximized my space in ways that I never would have imagined. For instance, he made the entrance to the dining room bigger. He placed the molding more on the ceiling than on the wall to lift the eye. He wallpapered the bedroom hallway, which I thought was an unnecessary extravagance. But Ford was right. It creates a separation of space and gives the area a different texture. Every day—seriously, every single day—I walk around the apartment and think how lucky I am to have Ford in my life."

—LINDA WELLS

Approaching a ROOM

THROUGH AN UNASSUMING ENTRANCE AND TYPICAL LOBBY,
up a nondescript elevator, and down a hall (similar to that of
any number of Manhattan apartments) lies the singular home of
photography agent Jordan Shipenberg. Walking through the front
door is like stepping into the past and the future at the same time.
At first, the vast space appears monochromatic, but as your eyes
adjust to the light (so much light), it reveals an abundance of pale
colors—grays, black, and white. And, even though it is enormous
for a New York residence, the room is inviting and calming rather
than cool or off-putting.

Originally three narrow apartments, Shipenberg's apartment
could easily have become a warren of interconnected rooms, but
Huniford saw it as a unified oasis, reminiscent of 1970s Ward
Bennett in the Hotel Chelsea lofts and updated in a way that is
prescient rather than backward-looking. To achieve this, walls
were removed, columns added, and skylights installed. Furniture
is placed in clusters so that each area feels discrete but connects to
the others by a unified palette. Shelving and staircases seem to float
on the walls, refusing to interfere with the overall lightness. Everything—including artwork, some by Shipenberg—has been arranged
with great precision, yet the order induces a feeling of relaxation.

<< This intimate seating area
was originally a cramped
second bedroom. A wall was
removed, opening the space
to the living room and making
it into a second conversation
area. The painting above the
custom sofa is by Linc Thelen.

> Harrison chaises from the
Huniford Collection flank a
custom screen wrapped in
bark paper in the Shipenberg
living area. The concrete
cylinder is both a floating
pedestal and side table.

Seating areas are spread out like
private islands in a sea of pale
neutrals, celadon, gray, and white
in the Shipenberg living space.
A Franklin sofa, Barrow chairs
(left) and a Thompson chair (right)
from the Huniford Collection
surround a custom coffee table.

The key to Huniford's approach to layout and furnishings is that his interiors are never too crowded. He is careful to maintain flow and sight lines and not to spoil a room with too many chairs or side tables. Gestures can be grand and impactful, but they are never meant to overwhelm.

Everything in the room has to maintain equilibrium. Ford avoids too-composed vignettes or precious moments that distract from the overall statement. And while he doesn't shy away from pattern, texture, or color, they are used with care and never for a superficial "wow" moment.

In Tribeca, a client (and old friend) who was redoing her home asked her architect to design a kitchen and separate dining room, believing this more traditional arrangement suited the way she lived and entertained. When Ford saw the plans, he asked her if she wouldn't prefer an eat-in kitchen, understanding that she and her family weren't, when it came down to it, "formal people." He diplomatically convinced her that she, in fact, would benefit from something more casual. The combined room became the star part of the apartment, a huge space filled with light where everyone—both family and guests—ends up spending most of their time.

For a family home in the Hamptons, Ford and his team similarly combined three small rooms into a multifunctional space, revealing beams and raising the ceiling in the process. Originally, the route went from the cramped kitchen to a smallish dining room to a comfortable but not generous living area. Once combined, each of these areas now feels generously proportioned even though each is roughly the same square footage as before. To further the effect, the kitchen was stripped of some "sad" bits (carpeting, old cabinets) and everything was either painted white or replaced by something white, such as the marble countertops.

Huniford arranges furniture to maximize the possibilities of both private living and entertaining family and friends. Long benches, couches, and banquettes are roomy enough for one person to stretch out on or four (or more) people to sit on comfortably at the same time. Armchairs, hard-backed chairs, ottomans, chaise longues, and other perches allow two or three people within a larger group to form their own temporary worlds, rejoining the others when ready. Rooms seem to feel exactly the right size whether you're alone or sharing them with a dozen other people.

The L-shaped kitchen of Aaron and Alana Feldman, now cleared of built-in cabinets, carpet, and wallpaper, has white countertops that, in combination with the new white wood cabinets, high-mounted lights, and painted floors, create a wonderfully spacious feeling.

In the Nashville living room,
a curved custom sofa and an
unusually shaped table con-
nect the seating options in this
very large space. The sofa's
curve is enveloping, while the
irregular edges of the teak
tree trunk coffee table in an
ebony shellac extend toward
the armchairs.

> This den in Bridgehampton is a multifunctional room for family time. Here Huniford once again blurs the line between what is precious and what is not. A streamlined sofa with nubby linen slipcover is accompanied by a 1940s chair from Saint-Tropez and a white plaster column lamp with a mica shade. A series of Agnes Martin drawings hang on the wall; the sculpture is by John Steck.

>> The two-on-one placement of custom armchairs and a nineteenth-century barrel chair in this Connecticut living room is classic, giving options for the ways in which people can interact. On the side tables, patinated brass columnar lamps are juxtaposed with industrial objects.

< In the library in North Salem, a large, leather-wrapped top sitting on a pair of metal saw-horses is deceptive. Both its height and that of the armchairs are raised so players can sit up straight while still feeling cozy. The painting is by Jonathan Meese.

∧ In Jeffrey Seller's office in midtown Manhattan, materials and textures are unusually rich, creating a comfortable environment that is more like a home than an office. Ludlow ottomans from the Huniford Collection and a pedestal table face a painting by Bryan Edgar. The crystal ball is made of watch parts and gears cast in resin.

In the lobby/seating area of a Manhattan hair salon, a long space was unified by an equally long custom-built sofa. A painter's drop cloth is stretched like a canvas above. Small concrete tables on wheels and lightweight chairs provide flexible seating.

The variety of shapes and periods of the chairs and sofa in this 1950s Upper East Side living room (originally designed by Gordon Bunshaft) creates a feeling of ease and intimacy in the expansive space. Furnishings include a pony skin rug, a Josef Hoffmann chair, and a writing table inspired by Donald Judd. Two of the chairs are covered in a linen from Nantucket Looms. The painting is by Joshua Avery Webster.

< In an Upper East Side living room, a custom ottoman functions both as seating and as a table, creating a unique configuration with a pair of nineteenth-century white-washed Louis XV-style chairs in front of the fireplace. The landscape on the right is by John Alexander.

> In the Shipenberg guest bedroom, right angles and flat surfaces play with the abundant light from the nearby window. Smaller objects (art-work and patinated machine parts and weights on bedside table) keep everything in balance.

< John Gore's office evokes a gentlemen's club with a bit of history. Worn leather and dark wood provide plenty of gravitas while still being welcoming. A custom frame clad in leather surrounds a mirror that is also a TV screen. The coffee table attributed to Bagues.

>> A metal bamboo daybed inspired by Adnet and a 1940s-inspired chair covered in blue horsehair sit on a handwoven Swedish rug in an Upper East Side living room. A print by David Hockney hangs between 1940s Venetian scones above the mantel.

< An L-shaped banquette lines the walls of the dining nook with cerused-oak floors off a West Village kitchen. The table is hammered copper with a back-painted glass top. Above are a drawing by Dan Miller (left) and a print by Marcus Eek (right).

∧ A newly raised ceiling and brighter light make this combined space (it used to be three rooms) in the Hamptons feel much larger than it actually is. The living room opens directly to the kitchen, creating an overall sense of tranquility, reinforced by the white upholstery of the sofa and ottoman. The globe on the mantel is a vintage dishwasher rack, a foil to the Buccellati crab on the coffee table.

<< In Huniford's Tribeca kitchen, an open arrangement works well for both casual entertaining and cooking with his family and friends. Complementing the wire-brushed oak millwork and divider with bubble glass and metal muntins is a bronze Island, inspired by a Donald Judd worktable in the Marfa studio. The chair is by Jean-Michel Frank.

> Dormer bedrooms can have a cocoon-like feeling, as seen in this one in Connecticut. A crewel-work bedcover adds a layer of subtle color and texture that complements the cotton-velvet-upholstered headboard of the custom bed, layered with a mohair blanket. The side table was once used in a speakeasy; the bedside lamps were originally demijohns.

Scale and Proportion

"Every room feels 'right' and perfectly incorporates a balance of homey comfort and chic elegance. Ford's emphasis on scale and proportion guided all of our conversations with him as we designed our house. Throw pillows create inviting nooks on a long window seat, perfectly scaled light fixtures draw your eye upward to a soaring ceiling, sculptural pieces accent a long wall, and upholstered headboards lend serenity to the bedrooms. Oversized, custom, industrial ceiling fans balanced the rustic nature of our screened porch, and a beautiful and arresting metal dining table perfectly captured our love of entertaining in a classic but updated way."

—TAMARA J. F. SLOAN

STEPPING OUT OF THE BRIGHT AFTERNOON LIGHT AND THROUGH
the Nashville doorway of Carolyn and Del Bryant, into the lofty
entryway, there is only the slightest hint of the grand interiors that
lie beyond. The space is graceful but in no way glitzy. No tumes-
cent, jangly chandelier drips from the ceiling. There are no fussy
paint finishes that took a small army to achieve. Near an impressive
staircase is a simple bench covered in a wonderful fabric. More
immediate is the rattan console (if the word delicious could be
used about a piece of furniture, this would be the time) by Betty
Cobonpue that sits below a travertine-framed mirror by Maitland-
Smith. A pair of unassuming, but beautiful, pendant lamps
hang from the ceiling. The scale of the room and the furnishings
within it let you know you're somewhere awesome but do so in
a hushed voice.

Once inside, you'll find rooms of plush furniture with graceful
lines and exquisite fabrics, walls in a beguiling pale gray-green, and
singular objects worthy of an art gallery but here somehow look
inevitable. It's high design that doesn't want anyone to feel left
out. Each room is comfortable and welcoming, inviting guests to
immediately feel at home.

<< In a grand Bond Street
apartment in Manhattan,
Huniford designed an airy spiral
staircase, inserting elements
that are both sculptural and
playful—like climbing up into a
tree house. The petrified wood
bench displays a collection of
metal objects below a collection
of black-and-white photographs
by Peter Beard.

> The Nashville entrance hall
sets the stage for the cool
elegance to come, with a chic
assemblage on the right and
a comfortable bench. The wall
color—November Rain from
Benjamin Moore—creates the
perfect ambience. The Austrian
starburst pendants are by Emil
Stejnar.

Scale and proportion are central to Huniford's work, as important as color and fabric, perhaps even more so. His eye can immediately ascertain what a room needs to be and what it will take to achieve that. Rooms with good proportions need to have those maintained, while more awkward spaces can require a bit more sleight of hand to correct. Lower-ceilinged rooms, for instance, need lower seating; bold gestures can distract you in long, narrow rooms.

When it comes to using large-scale pieces, Ford believes in going full throttle. His beach house bedroom, for example, contains a large tree trunk and a giant ship's chain. These dramatic moments work because they fit within the context of an overall scheme, balanced out by others in the room. Sight lines are of great importance: where there is a focal point, there must also be a point of calm. The eye needs places to be drawn to and others where it is allowed to rest.

And the concepts of scale and proportion are not limited to ceiling heights and sofa lengths. They can touch on the emotional as well, such as creating that sense of expectation when a person walks into a home. Setting the stage without giving away the entire plot up front. Too much too soon leaves you with having to endlessly outdo yourself, which Ford believes inevitably leads to over-doing.

Even arrangements of flowers, leaves, and branches are a study in proportion–not the least of which the shape and height of the vessel. Blooms, branches, and stalks play off their containers to create a symbiosis. Ford's preference skews towards greenery, but he is nonetheless very handy with cut flowers. Whether they will be placed in the center of a large round table, tucked into the corner of a kitchen, or rest on the floor next to a desk are essential things to consider. The choice between a clutch of wildflowers in a small glass jar versus seven-foot-tall branches in a terra-cotta vase might seem as though it's only about the size of the space, but it's much more complicated—and rewarding—than it might initially seem.

An impressively grand arrangement in an alabaster vase sits on a nineteenth-century English leather-topped table in a Katonah master bedroom. The walls are covered in grass cloth.

In this Connecticut entryway, crisp chalky-white walls and rich wood tones create a strong graphic interplay. The mix of elegant furnishing includes an Austrian spoon-back chair and a stool attributed to Michael Taylor. Photographs by Irving Penn and Harry Benson hang by the front door. The oak floor is original to the early nineteenth-century house.

< At the base of this elegant spiral staircase in Amagansett is a 1940s French table, complemented by an early twentieth-century piano stool, an ottoman, and a geometric metal sculpture.

> In a Woodstock, New York, entry hall a cone-shaped mica pendant fixture designed by Huniford hangs over hangs over a Regency table and eighteenth-century American chairs.

A triptych by Jennifer Andrews unites this long room more effectively than a single piece of art, which could look undersized (or overwhelming). The sofa is upholstered in handwoven fabric from Nantucket Looms.

< A wood and rope ladder, formerly used on a ship, occupies the wall and helps to turn the armchair and side table into a discrete zone.

> This long hallway is punctuated on one side with multiple windows, which break up the tunnel-like feeling, as does the beamed ceiling. The large painting on the opposite wall is by Jack Pierson. The whale bone on the right marks the opening to the main living area.

>> This Martha's Vineyard porch has been transformed into a three-season space with screen doors and a fireplace. Two substantial sofas, an equally substantial table, and a hand-woven area rug establish a more private zone that feels intimate within the expansive space.

>> A smaller table placed in front of this banquette in Watermill creates a sense of closeness for those sharing the seating.

> A very large dining room in Marin County requires a very large table, this one from Oxford. The long benches create a communal spirit; they take the place of roughly a dozen chairs, which could seem chaotic. Floor covering is handwoven striped cotton by Elizabeth Eakins.

>> A nineteenth-century storage cabinet from a hardware store fills a long wall in the Marin County house. Italian wood and metal sconces, a series of elegant side chairs, and a simple, 20-foot-long farm table balance its mass, creating a uniquely beautiful multi-function area.

Flowers present an oppor-
tunity to break rules and to
play wlth scale and volume.
Huniford likes to create
drama with either oversized or
unexpectedly small arrangements, with unusual mixtures
of flowers, greenery, and
branches.

Landscape paintings transform this Upper East Side library and office into something that feels more like a room on a country estate. Walls were painted faux-bois, the rug is from Codemat, and armchairs are upholstered in Liberty of London velvet (left) and yellow horsehair (right).

A hand-troweled concrete-and-wood island and graceful stools give this Chelsea penthouse kitchen a lofty feeling. A trio of short, hanging pendants remain above eye level when sitting or standing at the counter. The woods of the cabinets, floor, and island complement one another and create unity. The wall hanging is by Sally England; prints to the right of the opening are by Robert Mangold.

< Rather than use a diminutive sofa in this smallish space, Huniford placed a built-in banquette along one wall, imparting a feeling of intimacy in the process. He then added smaller octagonal occasional tables and a cane armchair to balance the weight. A soft off-white wall color amplifies the restful ambiance.

∧ In this Martha's Vineyard dining room, a midcentury brass and mahogany table, upholstered chairs, and a sculptural banquette are paired with 1950s Italian hanging light fixtures. The backdrop is an installation of galvanized metal spools that cast a changing pattern of shadows throughout the day and the seasons.

Twin starburst fixtures hang over Early American beds in this Connecticut bedroom, creating a spare elegance. Bed pillows were made from patchwork quilts. The dhurrie rug is from India.

< An enormous bathroom in Watermill, New York, required everything to be over scaled, including the elegant double slipper tub. Objects such as the ladder-like rack on the wall help make the proportions of the room feel more human.

> The oversized chain found in the San Juan Islands (and carved from a single piece of wood) in Huniford's Bridgehampton bedroom plays with the idea of scale, as does the tree-trunk wall sculpture. These exaggerated pieces have the effect of mitigating the large size of the room, including the 16-foot ceiling height. Furnishings include an Italian brass bed and a nineteenth-century Klismos chair that once belonged to Bill Blass.

Materials

"I've known Ford for a couple of decades, and I think he has a very strong, singular vision. And his rooms are always very inviting. Each one is different, unique, special. With Ford, you can feel his hand, but the personality of the owner comes through. He has also had a life in the art world, is friends with artists, knows artists' work. He's in a certain way an artist himself. I think the aesthetic value is of the highest importance for him. He's in the thick of it. He knows what he wants. He is somebody who is actually curating the space."

—SUSAN DUNNE

and

ART

WITH A COLLECTION OF TWENTY MATISSE PRINTS ON THE WALL,

a designer might be tempted to tame the furnishings, creating a neutral envelope of whites, creams, and taupes against which the art could reign supreme. But Ford didn't want to play it safe for the lake house of close friends Jeffrey Seller and Josh Lehrer in North Salem, New York. Conversations with them in London years earlier had revealed a mutual appreciation for the Bloomsbury style of design and its Bohemian mix of art, materials, patterns, and colors. Ford wanted to create a classic American version. The result is a weekend house where their impressive art collection can coexist with an eccentric mix of floral wallpaper and upholstery, striped rugs, tufted leather, and natural pieces.

A soaring entryway was created during the gut renovation, a master bath upstairs relocated, and an office removed to form the two-story space. Upon coming through the front door, you see a large tree stump table and pair of rare Jean-Michel Frank stools paired with a huge vase of branches from the property. Flowers and greenery can be found throughout the house, arranged in midcentury or Swedish vases, some covered in charming floral patterns, or in ginger jars with traditional blue-and-white decoration.

Sofas in the living room are covered in two different patterns— one striped and one floral—that recur elsewhere in the house. Dignified, tufted leather armchairs play against the more exuberant prints. The dining table, originally in the adjoining room, was moved into the space, placed in front of the window overlooking the lake. This both fills out the very large room and create a more relaxed atmosphere.

<< A waterfall painting by Pat Steir is a bold backdrop in a Manhattan living space that includes a coyote-skin rug, a Jacques Quinet chair, and a table by Paul Frankl.

> Balancing the bold colors and patterns of Matisse's Jazz series are a rich brown leather and an unusual mix of appliqué stripe and printed floral fabric.

In a sitting room off the main living area, a large and comfortable sofa in an Italian brocade fabric is flanked by a pair of armchairs in yellow flower-print fabric. On the end tables are lamps in a Chinese stamp design with shades in a darker floral similar to that on the chairs. Another armchair in a patchwork pattern is near a bench upholstered in a graphic print. It all flirts with going too far but never does.

In the master bedroom, stripes again meet floral. The bed itself is covered in a ticking pattern, with an upholstered bench in a pink, gray, and green floral at the foot. On the adjacent wall, an oversized green canvas echoes the color of trees outside the windows. Even the bed cover, which was originally white, was dyed a subtle green.

Getting elements to balance—with or without an impressive art collection—is a matter of facilitating communication between them. It's a matter of client preference: do they prefer a hushed tête-à-tête or lively debate? Some people feel comfortable in one while the other might put their teeth on edge. Ford balances everything by listening to the volume of the conversation.

In quieter rooms, there is always something to break through the calm, and this is accomplished by varying textures and materials. A room that contains pale gray leather, velvet, and bouclé is decidedly more interesting than one where every piece is upholstered in the same gray linen. Even when the mood is formal, casual additions such as weathered wood side tables (especially painted and patinated) or an oxidized metal coffee table play against the properness. Rugs made from unusual materials—jute or coir, for instance—introduce an organic, relaxed feel, as do striped cotton dhurrie rugs, which are tidy but still Boho.

When rooms go bolder, it's about mixing a group of strong personalities that all get along. No one component can be so powerful that it completely dominates the others. A large sofa in a bold floral embroidery needs an equally charming and spontaneous partner (or two). When confident gestures are echoed—even subtly—elsewhere in a room, the effect is more cooperative than combative. Responding to one of the sofa's flower colors, for instance, and having an ottoman in a similar hue—even in a contrasting texture fabric such as a bouclé—creates this harmony. It's about high meets low: the porous wood of an antique cabinet near a silk-velvet upholstered bench; a few rugged pieces near more delicate, refined finishes. This provides fodder for a more interesting conversation.

In Katonah, a painting by Anselm Kiefer is paired with a chair by Eyre de Lanux.

< The high-back custom sofa, upholstered in mustard silk velvet, echoes the form of the Josef Hoffmann armchair, covered in a Hoffmann fabric by Maharam, but in a completely modern way. Behind are drawings by Jannis Kounellis. The bone coffee tables are by Enrique Gracel.

∧ In Huniford's Bridgehampton dining room, his sculpture of swordfish noses in a glass cloche is juxtaposed with a vase with seahorse handles found at a vintage shop in Paris.

In the Foxman/Cardet-Hernandez apartment, a highly eclectic combination of color, material, pattern, and period works because each piece is strong, making the interaction lively but not contentious. A tufted sofa with sleek arms is flanked by custom side tables and vintage ceramic lamps. A swivel leather armchair and a pair of chrome side chairs covered in cowhide complete the seating. The lamp bases are Northern California pottery. Photographs above the sofa are by Robert Mapplethorpe; the Ruler beside the window is by Huniford.

< In the entry hall of the Duka apartment, Lonnie Duka's slides line one wall and a shooting practice target hangs on another. In contrast, a graceful pink stool sits below. The custom rug reflects the graphic nature of the slides.

∧ In the Watermill guest bedroom, an assortment of nineteenth-century grain sieves scales the wall. On an early American drop-leaf table, more industrial equipment—a metal grain scoop and gear chain— and a Moroccan lamp. The cotton carpet is by Elizabeth Eakins.

∧ This Upper East Side
bedroom is filled with luxurious
materials that include a custom
bed covered in silvery musk
cotton velvet with a cream
colored rug and overlay of
a cowhide. White marble
table lamps contrast with the
concrete drum side table.
The painting is by Kelly Stuart
Graham.

> In a space with bold contem-
porary windows, a worn leather
chair and an arts and crafts
hexagonal table bring warmth
and a sense of history. The wall
sculpture is by Jill Weinstock.

∧ In the Duka master bedroom, large, dark photographs by Lonnie Duka envelop the room, the faces able to be interpreted as guardians or interlopers. The bed feels restful and colorful by contrast. On the bedside table are vintage molds on stands and a lamp made of a repurposed sonar reflector.

> A wall sculpture by Louise Nevelson entitled *Mirror-Shadow XXIX* is installed above a waterfall table by Jean-Michel Frank.

English walnut chairs, a
nineteenth-century wine
tasting table, and an Italian
light fixture from the 1940s
blend seamlessly with modern
Roman shades and a trio of
drawings by Ellsworth Kelly.
The floors are linoleum
but in an unexpected blue
and white.

∨ Barkpaper adds a subtle texture in the bedroom walls. Drawings over the bed were commissioned from Joseph Shetler. The custom bedside table is wrapped in linen and lacquered.

> The interplay of texture in this NoHo kitchen is both sophisticated and calming, a reflection of the city outside and the homeowner's desire for something low impact and more organic. Cabinets are faced in rustic wood reclaimed from a barn in Vermont. Metal doors, salvaged from a nearby Tribeca factory, a concrete countertop, and vintage Spanish stools add to the mix.

∧ Furnishings in this Watermill
den include a 1940s Roger
Capron ceramic coffee table,
a mahogany campaign-style
partners desk, smoky plexiglass
shell chairs, and a bronzed-
metal side table in the style
of Andre Arbus. A series of
aviation blueprints from the
1930s and 1940s lines the
walls.

> A rubble-stone wall sup-
ports a richly textured work by
John Breed. The asymmetrical
placement creates tension
between the circular form and
the slender rectangle of the
fireplace opening. On the right
are works by Scott Campbell.

Bold gestures such as the large metal balloon mold on a wall in Huniford's bedroom in Tribeca are a signature. A vintage Tuareg rug and custom metal-and-wood bed add a different scale of texture. Cerused-oak bedside tables hold shagreen lamps. The lobster sculpture in the window is from Deyrolle in Paris.

< This vignette subtly
juxtaposes tones of gray in
fabric, wood, and silver gilt
to highlight each of their
textures.

> In the piano room in Jeffrey
Seller's New York office,
textures and patterns in the
Morton chair from the Huniford
Collection, a bone side table,
a lamp by Mads Capriani of
Denmark and found objects
quietly command attention.
The wall color and Roman
shades have a calming effect.
The photograph on the
windowsill is by Josh Lehrer.

On Martha's Vineyard, a
wide range of elements is
possible because nothing
is aggressively antique
or modern. A sofa in blue
linen and Stickley wicker
armchairs are matched with
a vintage leather pommel
horse, which acts like a
fourth wall. The metal lamp
and chandelier are softened
by a parchment mirror by
Karl Springer, a custom rug,
and wallpaper made from
pressed botanicals.

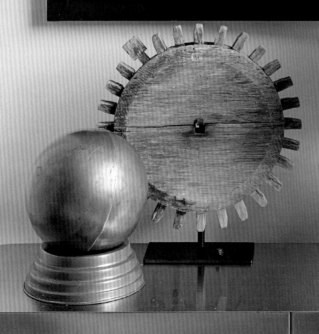

MIX
and
MATCH

"My partner, Josh Lehrer, and I just renovated a colonial clapboard house in North Salem. Ford, through his gorgeous interior design and thought, made it into a house we love. Ford is an artist. He is a sculptor with spaces. And he has a beautiful expression that is both comforting and cozy while also having artistic flair. And artistic difference. It's different from anything else. It has a point of difference. And he accomplishes that through sculptural ideas, through color, and, of course, through the beautiful textiles that he chooses."

—JEFFREY SELLER

WHEN DESIGNING A HOME IN LITCHFIELD COUNTY, CONNECTICUT

Huniford was given unusual freedom by his clients, who encouraged him to proceed, more or less unfettered, with his concept. He envisioned a dramatic tension between three major themes—the rough-hewn/rustic, the traditional/tailored, and the more sumptuous/decorous. This interplay was meticulously curated and results in an overall balance and harmony that never sacrifices one element for the others. Each is allowed to be expressed fully, accentuating the others in the process.

The envelope consists of rough-hewn beams framing smooth white plaster walls, a study in contrasts. In terms of materials and furnishings, Ford created a one-of-a-kind, highly evolved space that projects elegance without feeling the least bit off-putting. Fabrics—including one used by Albert Hadley twenty-five years ago in his own home—are tactile and inviting. Everywhere there are striking moments: bold blue-and-white bathroom floor tiles, floral fabrics on a bed frame, vintage maps on a bathroom's walls, Moroccan occasional tables beside contemporary armchairs to name a few. But a tranquil equilibrium is maintained through a palette of white, yellows, blues, neutrals as well as plenty of organic pieces.

<< In a Crosby Street master bedroom, earthy elements—wood, bronze, metal, clay—form a layered vignette. The vintage brushed stainless-steel cabinet forms the base for a wooden gear, ceramic lamp, metal orb, and base. A work by Robert Montgomery hangs above.

> The couple who own this house in Connecticut have a strong sense of adventure and were very open to design possibilities. An interplay between elements that are rustic, tailored, refined and sumptuous creates dramatic tension. The painted-wood settee is Swedish.

For a project in Watermill, New York, for Walter Bobbie and David Frye, Huniford mixed antiques, vintage pieces, and new upholstery into a retreat with a different take on the tension between rustic and refined. It's tasteful but not showy, formal at times but never stuffy. In the dining room, the curtains hang from a square rod mounted on the ceiling, and this more traditional detail plays against an eleven-foot bluestone table, antique chairs found in Paris and reupholstered in a Maharam fabric, and a custom pendant inspired by Viennese designer Josef Hoffmann. At the end of the table is a bullseye mirror that was originally part of an airplane engine. A guest room has twin antique bed frames and striped Pendleton blankets, a contemporary Swedish writing table and chair, and a spare, modern pen-and-ink drawing on the wall.

Huniford's particular ability is to bring together seemingly disparate elements into a harmonious arrangement. For a project on the Lower East Side, a somewhat industrial metal table is flanked by two benches upholstered in wool bouclé and a pair of molded-leather armless chairs. In the nearby living area, two curved armchairs in blush velvet, from his own line, sit near a Wiener Werkstatte hammered Seccession table. Uptown, a dining room features elegant striped silk wallpaper, more chaste embroidered linen curtains, a hammered brass-edge dining table and painted and gilded chairs beneath an ornate, multiarmed chandelier. On paper, these amalgams could sound discordant, but they are, in the end, entirely cohesive.

Ford has always incorporated furniture from different periods in his projects, using storied antiques side-by-side strikingly modern furnishings. He does not discriminate, although his eye is particularly drawn to Europe of the eighteenth and nineteenth centuries. That said, chipped, painted tables from the 1950s or a steel console from the 1970s is equally welcome. He also believes in collecting as an investment, and he encourages his clients to think the same way. Truly timeless pieces, as opposed to fashion- or trend-driven choices, can be reworked into new arrangements as tastes change over time.

In terms of the actual process of mixing and matching, he's the first to admit he has no real boundaries. Expensive and inexpensive, important and workaday, glossy polished walnut and scuffed ash—they can all coexist in the same room. To Ford, it is all about a point of view and confidence. You have to take chances and believe what works for your eye looks good.

< A handmade papier-mâché pendant lamp draped in fabric—inspired by Josef Hoffmann—hangs above a bluestone trestle table in the dining room of Walter Bobbie and David Frye in Watermill.

>> In the Connecticut sitting room, elegant armchairs upholstered in a Schumacher embroidered fabric by Elsie de Wolfe flank a contemporary bone and brass table beneath rough-hewn beams. The side table is made of fabric and resin; the chesterfield sofa is upholstered in antique French linen.

< In Nashville, a spectacular, curvy rattan console by Betty Cobonpue stands below a travertine mirror by Maitland-Smith. A faceted metal stool is grounded, in contrast to the marble Buddha floating above its base.

> In the double-height North Salem entry hall, a California Redwood root live-edge table holds Italian majolica ewers and a massive Murano glass vase filled with mountain laurel branches from the property. The stools on the left are vintage, inspired by Jean-Michel Frank.

In an elegant Upper East Side apartment, deeply tufted fabrics in pale floral brocade and rich coffee-and-caramel stripes complement the ochre walls and the muted shades of the heirloom carpet. A painting by Phillip Smith hangs above the custom sofa; to the right is a print by Michael Newhouse.

> In a Manhattan living area, the rectilinear pattern of the double-height window works with the angular lines of the Jacques Quinet and Josef Hoffmann armchairs. Some panels in the windows are frosted to break up the expanse of glass. The garden was designed by Mario Nievera.

< A Tribeca duplex loft shows that rooms can function in different ways from far away and from close up. At a distance, the furniture arrangement anchors the seating area within its lofty enclosure. Up close, the unified palette makes the area feel snug and convivial.

<< In this dynamic East Hampton living room, a painting by Deborah Kass (appropriating a Warhol image) is hung inches from an antique cranberry rake. Lamp is English basalt with a mica shade. The Chinese waterfall coffee table is paired with an early American primitive wood chair.

> In a Sag Harbor living room, works by Louise Nevelson, Sol LeWitt, Thomas Nozkowski, and Alfred Jensen mingle with Barclay lamps from the Huniford Collection, 1960s Italian armchairs, a custom sofa, and laboratory paraphernalia on the low table.

>> In the dining room in Nashville, chrome-frame Milo Baughman chairs are matched with a mahogany Louis XVI table. Window shades are Rubelli silk stripe from Donghia, while the custom bench is upholstered in persimmon velvet from Pollack. Poised above it all is an Italian brass chandelier. The painting over the mantel is by Richard Feaster.

>> United by their colors and visual textures, these objects from different worlds—a nineteenth-century Mexican cabinet, a chair by Jean-Michel Frank, a wall sculpture made from ceramic electrical elements mounted on wood—look entirely natural together. The drawing is by Robert Dash.

< Patterns are at play in this North Salem guest bedroom. The pillow is embroidered crewel from Marston House. Fabric on the Swedish white-washed bedframe is Isfahan Stripe from Peter Dunham. Lamps are découpage and roman shades are in Pasha Original from Penny Morrison Fabrics. A set of framed antique color thread charts above the bed complement the textiles below.

> In the North Salem entry hall, a vintage Swedish flat-weave rug is a modern counterpart to a nineteenth-century English side table and eighteenth-century French Jacob chairs with striped linen fabric. The metal vessel under the table is Japanese.

<< Curves of a wall piece by Claes Oldenburg, made of canvas coated with resin, cord, and string painted with latex and spray enamel, contrast with the rectilinear geometry of a Stickley-inspired table. The klismos chair is by Kaare Klint.

<< Colors and patterns from the past come together in a dynamic, modern way in the Connecticut guesthouse bedroom. An English flip-top table used as a desk is covered with vintage fabric that feels entirely fresh. The vintage stool, found in London, has a rope seat and back. The blanket on the bed is also vintage, but its pattern is intentionally mismatched to the desk to create something new.

< In the screened porch off the library in North Salem, a wicker sofa sits in the niche between two storage closets. Flanking the coffee table by Gordon Martz are a pair of stylish French art deco wicker chairs.

∧ In a Woodstock bedroom, an eighteenth-century Sheraton field bed, antique French linens, and nineteenth-century chest of drawers lie under the watchful eye of the owner's grandmother.

> Vintage Knoll chairs upholstered in a Lee Jofa Sunbrella fabric sit on a striped cotton kilim beneath an antique Belgian oak chandelier. Vintage propellers decorate a small console. A collection of onyx balls on top of an Italian marble game table suggest a lively match in progress.

Exploring

"We really wanted the palette to be as natural and as earthy as possible. Within that, Ford was able to create a subtlety, bringing out an incredible coziness and feeling that it comes from the earth—but also has color. We have some green and some celadon, which is drawn from nature. And our back stairs, for instance, are very colorful. He was able to help us work color in, but in a way that's subtle and that would last for a long time. After six months you wouldn't tire. It ages well. In fact, you like it even more as time goes on."

—SALLY SNIPES

COLOR

ALONG A LONG EXPANSE OF CENTRAL PARK WEST SITS A SERIES
of architectural gems in styles ranging from Neo-Renaissance and
Gothic Revival to Beaux-Arts and Art Deco. Developed between
the 1880s through the 1930s, they are decidedly grand, with ornate
lobbies and polished brass doors. Most are clad in unassuming pale
sandstone, beige or red brick, and/or terra-cotta, a neutral foil to
the lush green explosion a few yards away.

One imagines the apartments inside these structures to be a
world of Delft blue and cream chintz, and for many this is true.
In one such prewar building, however, Huniford created something
unique, taking this play of neutral stone color against a riot of
greens as a starting point and adding in layers of strong accent
color and texture. While the bones of the place might be traditional
—a large entry foyer, high ceilings, wood-burning fireplaces, and
oversized living areas—the resulting palette is anything but.

Furnishings are at times resolutely modern, while at others
reference the various styles of the neighboring buildings. Fabrics
provide unexpected departures with cleverly anachronistic use
of cerulean mohair, tangerine velvet, and chartreuse hair calf.
Some of these colors amplify those found in the graphic and non-
representational art, a top-flight collection.

<< In Connecticut, soft greens
in the long custom sofa and
printed Roman shades add a
significant amount of subtle
color. Hints of green are also
present in the framed maps
and the embroidered fabric on
the armchair.

> This dining room on Central
Park West has classical under-
pinnings, but it features more
audacious touches such as the
chartreuse leather cushions on
the chairs, which relate to the
Robert Kushner painting.

Pattern is to add even more visual richness, and where yet another color would be too much—subtle geometrics on rugs or simple florals on pillows. Overall, these confident touches provide energy but never overwhelm, carefully placed as they are among a palette of soft beiges, grays, and browns. A home is, ultimately, always to be a refuge and never a gallery.

Huniford has always been drawn to water and sky, woods and forests; as a result, he has a particular love of blues and greens. He grew up spending time at the Thousand Islands in Upstate New York where his family had a cottage. Often working outside, building rock walls for his mother's garden, he was immersed in nature, an exposure that informed the way he thinks about color and the way it changes and moves with the light throughout the day, the seasons, or with the weather: how everything could quickly become desaturated when a storm came in and vibrant again as the sun reappeared. Reminding him of his childhood, this range of colors always brings him back to a place of calm, clarity, and stillness.

Rooms—or an entire home—are frequently painted in shades that capture this mercurial sense of chromatic movement. Every wall in Ford's Bridgehampton house is a color he calls Foggy Summer Squall. (He loves whites that have been made a bit dusky with the addition of green and gray or blue and gray.) In other projects, he has used colors with names like Overcast, Nantucket Gray, Withersfield Moss, and Silken Pine. His palette is not by any means limited, however. Painters like Agnes Martin have always inspired him. Martin worked in a consistent range of pink, blue, and yellow to create rigorously geometric compositions. He adapted one client's request for the colors of the inside of a seashell to a sophisticated Martin-esque range. In an apartment on Cornelia Street, similar shades form a thread that runs throughout the space, instilling it with a sense of order and quietude.

Traveling through India, especially in sacred cities like Pushkar, Huniford developed an appreciation for the explosion of colors, from an earthy range of clay bodies and vessels to electric magentas and marigolds of flowers, spices, and cloth. He is judicious with these, and they often appear, as they do on Central Park, as artwork and accents rather than the basis of a palette. Sobriety meets unbridled celebration—a story told in color.

In the Upper East Side apartment of Linda Wells, a pair of armchairs in mustard velvet stand out against the pale green walls and deep greens of the painting by John Alexander. Striped window shades pick up tones from the chairs, while the striking 1930s English emerald-green glass sconces multiply shades from the painting.

< Small spaces are often decorated with demure patterns in timid color palettes. Not so in this powder room in North Salem, where bold floral wallpaper provides character. The not-quite-matching, see-through glass mirror by Fontana Arte ups the effect. These are paired with a hand-painted Danish terra-cotta vase by L. Hjorth and a saffron colored gingham skirt on the vanity.

> In this Tribeca apartment, subtle colors were selected from the bold painting and used in the decor. The mauve tones in the velvet quietly add contrast to the neutral palette surrounding them. Waxed-plaster walls in pale ochre create a luxe envelope.

> On Central Park West,
the flashes of green in an
Alex Katz print and in the
furnishings give this serene
palette a subtle jolt, creating
a slight tension that brings
energy with it. The stool has a
walnut-and-bone inlay frame
and the cushion is upholstered
in olive pony skin.

>> On Martha's Vineyard,
the soft blue of a built-in
banquette—as well as that of
the silvery blue in the Fortuny
pillows—is perfect foil for
the rough-hewn beams. The
botanicals pressed into the
wallpaper reference the
beams, albeit in a delicate
way.

>> In the Marin County entry,
color is layered to feel very
casual, but it has been carefully thought out. The honey
wood of the staircase and
floor work with the pigmented
plaster walls and the inlaid
cream-colored floor tile. The
olive seats, marigold flowers,
and spray of greenery are
both contesting and organic.

The owner of this Chelsea apartment bordering the High Line preferred tactility over color. The group of highly touchable fabrics and furnishings are at once similar yet remarkably different, including vintage chairs and lamps and a custom sofa, ottoman, coffee table, and side tables.

< In this vignette, the symmetry of the cabinet with its central blue doors flanked by white plays off an asymmetrical arrangement of a tall charcoal drawing by David Schofield paired with a small sculpture by Doug Rochelle (left), a rounded vase, and a second sculpture by Philippe Hiquily.

> The playful Bloomsbury-inspired colors of the risers of the backstairs in Marin County are a lighthearted touch.

>> The enormous dining area of a Crosby Street loft feels more congenial because of the combination of 1950s Gunlocke chairs and custom benches, all upholstered in a rich mulberry velvet that works well with the brickwork yet is very striking on its own. Over the table is a 1950s chandelier by Alvin Lustig for Lightolier.

< Sometimes a prominent color can simply exist, unreferenced, as seen in this dining space where the blue of the windows was not repeated in the custom table and benches. Instead, a palette of steel, gray, and beige peacefully coexists alongside it. Custom dining benches are covered in curly lamb's wool.

> Soothing watercolor blues and greens come together in this Martha's Vineyard kitchen, where they appear as leather chairs, flowers, pottery—even cookware. It's a way to introduce color and still keep it subtle.

A master bedroom in Katonah takes inspiration from the paintings of Agnes Martin. The mix of neutrals, pale yellow, pale blue, and light brown is understated but rich. An antiqued four-poster brass bed and a 1940s Venetian mirror add reflective contrast as do the brass accents of the nineteenth-century commode, fitted with a marble top and used as a dresser.

In Watermill, austere twin
beds, originally in a convent,
are covered in brown and
beige Pendleton blankets that
suggest summer camp, but
the Italian, Prouvé-inspired
desk and chair are definitely
grown up. Celadon walls
and rug create a serene
enclosure, and a simple black-
and-white drawing by Paul
Edmonds completes the look.

In the California living room, an ice-blue sofa both anchors the large space and provides a genteel color moment within the more organic surrounding tones of hewn wood, wrought iron, and natural stone. Chocolate-brown Spanish provincial lamps complement the coppered coffee table.

Changing Rules, SOLVING PROBLEMS

"Ford is a master at bringing the outside in, without ever making a space feel homespun. Whether in the country or in the city, Ford has been able to make our homes feel at one with nature, incorporating just the right blend of textures, colors, and designs."

—ARIEL FOXMAN

BORDERING THE HIGH LINE IN CHELSEA, A MANHATTAN RESIDENCE
is wrapped in glass, with a very long main space that spans the full length of the apartment. The clients, a couple with adult children who frequently visit, requested an absence of color as the palette. Their lifestyle required a plan that could just as easily work for a large dinner party as a quiet evening at home for the two of them. So Huniford had to devise a way to both celebrate the layout with its abundant light and space while simultaneously forming a relaxing and functional haven.

The solution is an elegantly furnished balance of white, cream, beige, and gray—with touches of light wood as gentle contrast—in a curvy yet streamlined sort of anti-city. He worked with the architect to break up the long line of the main area without adding walls. An angular fireplace in cast concrete was installed, providing a way to divide without conquering. It is open on both sides—allowing flow—but still forms two distinct zones. On one side is the living area; on the other, a family area with open kitchen and dining room.

<< Under the high ceilings of this Manhattan living area, a large octagonal mirror draws in the picturesque garden outside and makes the room feel less imposing, the seating area more intimate. Chocolate leather floors with hand-stitched seams are as luxurious as the furnishings. The armchair is by Jacques Quinet.

> In this apartment along the High Line in Chelsea, a floor-length space is divided by a poured concrete fireplace inspired by an Ellsworth Kelly sculpture, with a living area on one side and family/dining areas and kitchen on the other. Because it floats with space on either side, the fireplace provides separation but does not interrupt the light and flow.

FOR
YOUR
IN
FOR
MATION
WE
THE
PEOPLE
ARE
ALL
IMMIGRANTS

VALENTINO FRAMES AND VARIATIONS

THE IVY LEAGUE DANIEL CAPPELLO ASSOULINE

AN ORIGINAL
70 Years of Innovation and Play ASSOULINE

AFRICAN DRESS

ULTIMATE LANDSCAPE DESIGN

The Private World of Yves Saint Laurent & Pierre Bergé

A TOUCH OF style

The Night Before BAFTA

TUFTE · VISUAL EXPLANATIONS

STYLISTS NEW FASHION VISIONARIES

Elsewhere in the apartment, furnishings are sculptural but not heavy handed. There is a distinct lack of ornamentation, trim, or fussiness. Bright color has been replaced by a rich use of texture and surface. The eye is continuously delighted but not distracted. It's definitely urban and highly sophisticated, but every inch of it looks like somewhere you can curl up and feel comfortable, safe, and at ease.

The opposite challenge occurs with very large spaces. Their scale can make them difficult to approach. It's about creating a rhythm, punctuating along the way with seating areas (sometimes Ford will put two in a long living area to break it up) or layer a living area with a dining area, a combination that brings a particular warmth with it. Spaces in which multiple activities occur are somehow primordial, at once efficient and comforting.

Wide hallways, for instance, are often overlooked, but can be transformed from being simply a passageway to include a small office, an art gallery, the place for a bench on which to sit briefly. A subset of this is the vast bathroom, which can feel institutional and cold if left too bare. Decorative objects on the walls provide an immediate sense of intimacy. A large clawfoot tub placed away from the walls or corners is both a solution to using up space and creating an island of serenity.

Large apartments and houses can also possess long expanses of empty walls. Placing artwork on them is an obvious choice, but so are found objects, especially when arranged in groupings. These provide a break for the eye as it moves along, distractions like punctuation marks in a long sentence.

And creating an oasis is especially important for urban clients. City dwellers fortunate enough to have enviable views can nonetheless find themselves in a love/hate relationship. The qualities that make these views exciting also makes them distracting, constantly demanding attention. Ford deals with this by avoiding primary seating areas facing toward the windows. In fact, the sofa often has its back to the them, allowing a respite from the bustle outside. He also counters the geometry of the architecture with curves, soft fabrics, and a tranquil palette.

This sideboard is a cityscape unto itself and brings urban energy to the interiors of the Foxman/Cardet-Hernandez apartment. Earthenware vases are from Czechoslovakia. The painting between the windows is by Maynard Monrow.

> This passageway in the Shipenberg apartment was turned into a functional space that can be used as an office or a casual dining area. The custom trestle table and banquette and the mid-century leather sling chairs by William Katavalos for Laverne International are industrial but chic.

>> In a space with glazed walls and panoramic views, a long bench and console table in pale neutrals manage the scale and create a restful atmosphere that allows for the absence of typical softening elements such as window treatments or an area rug. In the spare space, nubby fabrics add texture. The black-and-white print is by Willy Ronis.

< In Linda Wells's Upper
East Side apartment, a curved
settee takes the place of
chairs at the Louis XVI mahogany table. The botanical print
fabric by Liberty of London
plays against the stripes of
the Roman shades.

∧ This seating area off a
kitchen features a built-in
banquette upholstered in
leather, an early twentieth-
century child's chair, and a
Donald Judd wall sculpture.

In vast loft spaces such as this
one on Crosby Street, it can
be a challenge to make the
space feel intimate. Creating
two separate seating areas
(there is another to the left)
helps manage scale as does
the round rug, which softens
the boxiness of the large
room. Keeping everything low
also facilitates coziness. The
Papa Bear chair is by Hans
Wegner; the armchair in gray
curly lamb was inspired by
Jean Royère. The painting is
by John Codling.

∧ In the North Salem master bedroom, a tufted blue-leather couch is paired with two Egyptian-inspired wood stools, used here in place of a coffee table. On the nineteenth-century painted table is a 1960s brass lamp with a custom shade.

> Oddly shaped rooms can be hard to make feel cozy. By using a round rug and rounded furnishings in a range of soothing grays, this seating area becomes a welcoming refuge. The sofa, coffee table, armchairs, and side table are by Huniford. A custom Cork cabinet is tucked into the narrowest point of the room, blunting the point of the triangular space.

> Even though they live in a large apartment, the owners of this Manhattan aerie did not want to experience every moment on a huge scale. The dining table, designed by Huniford, opens up to seat fourteen, but it spends most of its time in this configuration, more suited to family dinners. Hanging above is an alabaster chandelier by Atelier Alain Ellouz.

>> In the Crosby Street loft, a custom resin bar in persimmon is adjacent to the kitchen, creating the contrast of a utilitarian working kitchen next to a moment of high glamour. Above is a cloud piece by Stanford Biggers, a daring placement of white art against a white wall.

In the entry hall of the Schiff family home in Sagaponack, the converted potato barn retains its wide pine floorboards. An English oak table stands in front of a seating nook, which takes the place of a freestanding bench. The blue botanical wallpaper is by Clarence House, turning it into a beautiful sitting area. The single barn door at the hall's end is an intentionally unharmonious moment, meant to reference the original structure.

< The powder room in the Crosby Street loft features Andy Warhol mylar paper patterned with a crowd scene in a copper finish. A poured-concrete basin is inset into an industrial blue metal worktable to serve as a vanity.

> Curated objects—a plaster candelabra attributed to Giacometti and a silver-and-bone tray—allow the master bathroom in Huniford's Tribeca loft to remain simple and calming but still resonate. The tub has a low profile to fit beneath the tall window, which is covered with a screen of vintage shutters that slide into a pocket.

The cupboard and drawers
next to the fireplace were
added to provide storage for
linens, books, and small items.
With plenty of breathing room
and not an abundance of furnishings, the cubby-like area
beneath the slanted ceiling
feels cozy. Rather than install
a traditional mantel, Huniford
designed a native stone
surround for the fireplace.

Authenticity

"Ford has a singular ability to understand people and how they live. He is able to create unique spaces that are about great design, practicality, and function. We recently collaborated on a project together that reflects my personality, point of view, and sensibility. His ability to navigate different aesthetics enables him to always create special and individual spaces for clients."

—JOHN GORE

and

HARMONY

HUNIFORD VALUES HIS HOME ABOVE ALL. "IT IS IMPORTANT THAT
my home be comfortable—for me, my family, and my friends,"
he says. "It is that—but it's also a laboratory, a place to experiment
with the way fabrics and objects with an artisanal character feel
alongside more refined ones. It's about taking elements from different periods and not letting their history affect how you use them,
but instead finding a shared harmony."

When he entertains, Ford likes to invite a group of people
of various occupations, ages, backgrounds, thereby leaving it to
chance who might click, become a couple, get into an argument,
or go into business together. All have happened. When designing a
home, his process is much more deliberate, although the outcomes
can be equally magnetic.

In the vacation home of Tamara and Adam Sloan on Martha's
Vineyard, Ford's bent for mixing vintage pieces with found objects
and modern furnishings can be seen at practically every turn.
Throughout the house, pieces such as decades-old Moroccan
café tables, decorated with a mysterious set of colorful symbols
burnished and softened by time, rub elbows with newer, more
understated ones, each player highlighting what is interesting and
unique about the other.

<< In the otherwise sleek and
modern Shipenberg apart-
ment, a cow sculpture made
of reclaimed wood and dis-
played on a pedestal becomes
a sort of talisman. The open
staircase brings light into the
expansive concrete space.

> A quartet of alternating,
vintage oars turns this
stairwell—a typically neglected
area—in Martha's Vineyard
into a graphic reference to
the island's history of whaling
and fishing. The window
was found in another local
historic house and installed
here, bringing light into the
otherwise dark passage.

A variation on this idea occurs at the upstate New York home of Jeffrey Seller and Josh Lehrer, where a particularly striking meeting of color, pattern, and form casts a spell. It's difficult to imagine any of the individual components not being there. Graphic modern art, ornate and floral embroidered fabrics, quirky Chinese and Dutch ceramics used as lamp bases, and earthy sea grass rugs might sound on paper as if they might not come together as logical scheme, but it's the controlled eccentricity that makes it exceptional.

When the basic scheme is sleek and very modern, as it is with the Shipenberg loft in Manhattan, carefully curated and well-placed natural wood pieces and vintage found objects provide just the right degree of earthiness. Similarly, in a brick-lined loft on Crosby Street, large-scale and unusual vintage furniture pieces and a backlit resin bar—designed by Huniford—create a clubby atmosphere that suits the tech executive who resides and frequently entertains here.

Combining furnishings to create a bit of tension is a concept at the core of Huniford's work. A velvet-clad, tailored sofa looks very different next to a smooth concrete side table than it would among other pieces of a similar style, period, and glamor level. The same can be said for his choice in art—including personal favorites Robert Rauschenberg and Ellsworth Kelly, whose color, texture, and sense of restraint can add to the interplay. But he also supports a range of contemporary and emerging artists.

Ford's ability to identify potentially disparate pieces that ultimately have this resonance—and to plot where they all will have the most impact—is well known to his clients. He collects with a curatorial eye and has an uncanny ability to identify unique objects that stand out for their particularly sculptural shape, unusual coloration, or singular personality.

Nothing is left to chance and everything is important in the creation of one of his truly authentic homes. It is also about taking risks and resisting the norms of mainstream design to create something never seen before.

< An vintage Italian card-table from Milan is a focal point in the North Salem library. Patinated bookshelves with pottery and ceramics were combined to create a pleasantly worn atmosphere, a contrast to the contemporary painting by Lisa Yuskavage.

>> In Huniford's Tribeca living room, he experiments with subtle colors, an abundance of textures, and varying levels of high and low. Furnishings include a custom sofa, a vintage chair that once belonged to Bill Blass, lamps by Bernard Rooke, and parchment nesting tables by Jean-Michel Frank. The wall sculpture above the sofa was designed by Huniford and fabricated by Nick Colbert.

< In this vignette, a French ceramic lamp from the 1940s is combined with a nineteenth-century American painted farm table and an industrial hanging fixture. The wood plank floor and ceiling beams retain the rustic gracefulness of this 100-year-old potato barn.

> In the den of his Bridgehampton house, Huniford once again blurs the line between what is precious and what is not. Here, a set of wooden skirt hoops is placed across the back wall. A chair covered in traditional woven cane sits near a giant ball made of thick twine. The coffee table is a graphic assemblage of tree trunk slices in tile.

< The long main corridor of this Crosby Street loft is a sort of museum of curiosities, including a vintage sliding board installed on the wall, center table by Romeo Rega set beneath a Luigi Caccia Dominioni chandelier, and tufted leather nineteenth-century butler's chair. Niches along the opposite wall hold a trove of found objects, pottery, candlesticks, and—of course—books.

> In the North Salem living room, a series of Matisse prints, a well-worn vintage leather armchair, and vintage sofas in a mix of fabrics reinforces the English Bohemian tone. A sculpture by Richard Tuttle sits on the dining table.

>> In the Watermill living room, a carefully edited mix of antique, vintage, and new pieces feel like an assemblage that happened slowly and naturally over time. Mica-shade columnar lamps share the space with a rustic farm table and a pendant light made from oxidized metal panels. The resin box sculpture is by Huniford.

< A door mounted on the ceiling in a hallway in Bridgehampton, near a trio of vintage maps and a worn box are a striking moment. In addition to providing character, the door hides an access panel to the attic. The wall triptych is terrain maps of Eastern Long Island. The handrail is early American.

> In the living space of the Crosby Street loft, coffee table from Hollywood set designer Billy Haines is a perch for links from an antique metal chain, an overtly industrial moment in this generally cozy space.

< A dozen carved wood
African shields climb the
dining area wall in a Cornelia
Street apartment, adding
graphic texture. The area is
too small—and the wall curved
and enclosing—for a single,
larger and bolder piece.
A custom banquette and a
Charles chair from the
Huniford Collection provide
the seating.

∧ In the Katonah dining room
of Bruce and Liz Fiedorek,
a patchwork goat hair rug
lends texture below the highly
polished French mahogany
dining table. The dining chairs
are attributed to Rhulmann. On
the walls are an eighteenth-
century Venetian mirror over
the mantel and a painting by
Adolph Gottlieb on the right.

<< In the Crosby Street master bathroom, a set of grain sifters spread out randomly across the wall create a sculpture that is graphic without being rigid.

<< Objects don't always have to be "logical" to bring a sense of drama. Such is the case with this pairing of a propeller and repurposed pommel horse in the Crosby Street master bedroom. They transform a large, plain wall into something of an art installation. Cork wallpaper behind the bed brings organic texture into this Manhattan loft.

> A gnarl of wood and a pair of grain sifters provide intense visual contrast to the pristine, monochromatic atmosphere in the Shipenberg apartment. They lend earthiness to the austerity, provide texture, and look like the works of art they are in the gallery-like space.

Acknowledgments

Creating this book has been an incredible experience, one I was able to accomplish thanks to the support of my family and friends. I would especially like to thank Andrew Gordon, who always inspired and encouraged my creativity. Thank you to my clients for their continued enthusiasm and trust—and for allowing me to photograph their homes. Thanks to my editor, Elizabeth White, for her faith and encouragement, and to graphic designer Rita Sowins for making everything look beautiful. To principal photographer Matthew Williams for his keen insight and ability to capture my vision with his camera. To Anthony Iannacci for his early support of this idea. Thank you to the writers and editors who have covered my work over the years. To the artists, photographers, architects, craftspersons, and everyone whose contributions bring these projects to life. Thanks to my design studio team–past and present–for their incredible dedication. Special thanks to Daniel LeBlanc for his steadfast and razor-sharp focus in coordinating all aspects of the book. Thank you to Pilar Viladas for the kind and thoughtful introduction. And thanks to Stephen Treffinger for his brilliant insight in putting my creative work into words.

Photography Credits

Principal photography by Matthew Williams
2, 4, 6, 8, 15, 16, 18, 20, 21, 22, 24, 28, 29, 32, 36, 37, 39, 40, 43, 44, 49, 52, 53, 56, 57, 58, 60, 62, 64, 72, 76, 78, 80, 82, 88 left, 88 right, 89 left, 89 right, 90, 94, 95, 99, 103, 104, 107, 108, 110, 113, 114, 115, 116, 122, 125, 126, 128, 137, 138, 140, 147, 148, 149, 150, 152, 155, 159, 160, 162, 163, 164, 166, 170, 172, 174, 175, 176, 184, 186, 190, 192, 194, 195, 198, 202, 203, 206, 209, 210, 212, 215, 216, 217, 220, 221, 222, 223, 224, 225, 226

Gieves Anderson: 92, 118, 168, 183, 188, 196
Max Kim Bee: 30, 31, 48, 71, 84, 86, 136, 146, 167, 171, 179
Pieter Estersohn: 55, 112
Genevieve Garruppo: 54
Robyn Lea: 83, 98, 111, 120, 124, 132, 178, 218
Tim Lenz: 34, 50, 66, 74, 96, 131, 134, 151, 156, 204
Nick Johnson: 26, 68, 81, 100, 106, 119, 121, 141, 144, 180
Tara Striano: 46, 63
Eric Striffler: 200, 214
Simon Upton: 142
William Waldron: 12, 38, 77, 154 191
Ryan Moore: 229

Library of Congress Control Number: 2020935581

ISBN: 978-158093-517-3

Design: Rita Sowins / SowinsDesign

Printed in China

The Monacelli Press
65 Bleecker Street
New York, New York 10012